T0196599

SAVE YOURSELF & SAVE THE PLANET

1001 GREEN & FUN LIFE HACK TIPS

*"Join the hippest new movement to rock
your world and our planet!"*

JUDY WONG DOBBERPUHL

WWW.SAVEYOURSELF.TIPS

BALBOA PRESS

A DIVISION OF HAY HOUSE

Balboa Press books may be ordered through booksellers or by contacting:

Balboa Press
A Division of Hay House
1663 Liberty Drive
Bloomington, IN 47403
www.balboapress.com
1 (877) 407-4847

Because of the dynamic nature of the Internet, any web addresses or links contained in this book may have changed since publication and may no longer be valid. The views expressed in this work are solely those of the author and do not necessarily reflect the views of the publisher, and the publisher hereby disclaims any responsibility for them.

The author of this book does not dispense medical advice or prescribe the use of any technique as a form of treatment for physical, emotional, or medical problems without the advice of a physician, either directly or indirectly. The intent of the author is only to offer information of a general nature to help you in your quest for emotional and spiritual well-being. In the event you use any of the information in this book for yourself, which is your constitutional right, the author and the publisher assume no responsibility for your actions.

Any people depicted in stock imagery provided by Thinkstock are models, and such images are being used for illustrative purposes only. Certain stock imagery © Thinkstock.

Printed in the United States of America.

ISBN: 978-1-5043-2577-6 (sc)
ISBN: 978-1-5043-2578-3 (e)

Library of Congress Control Number: 2014922772

Balboa Press rev. date: 12/31/2014

THANK YOU

I am grateful for every single person and sentient being that has taught me about making the most of this journey we call life. In a world of polarities, it's about embracing the happiness and sadness, the dark and the light, the love and the hate, the synchronicities and the mis-ques, the magic and the mundane.

This book is dedicated to my dear loving husband Ken. You can always make me laugh and appreciate the amazing love, fun and adventure that we continue to share together.

Thanks to my terrific family and friends for your constant love and support. The journey continues.

CONTENTS

1001 GREEN & FUN LIFE HACK TIPS

1. Grow your own organic veggie garden. Purchase Non-GMO heirloom seeds if you can.

2. Eat more greens. Get creative. More salads. More green smoothies. More goodness. More chlorophyll.

3. Drink at least 2-3 liters of water a day. More, if you exercise vigorously and if you live in high altitude.

4. Smile more and help others to smile. Everyone smiles in the same language.

5. Get more sleep. Know how much your body needs and get the rest you deserve and need.

6. Follow your passions.

7. Sing more during the day and not just in the shower. Singing raises your vibrations and the earth's.

8. Laugh daily.

9. Feed the homeless. Do what you can to help people that do not have clothing, shelter, food and water.

10. Volunteer at the local animal shelter.

11. Donate monthly.

12. Cook and clean for a friend or neighbor that might need help.

13. Learn about the food "pleasure trap" and why humans crave sugar, salt and fat and how you can better understand this epidemiology and how you can learn to make better food choices and why.

14. Learn to play a musical instrument…it is never too late to learn anything.
15. Do yoga daily.
16. Learn a new language…maybe several.
17. Go vegan or vegetarian. Learn why this is the compassionate way of life, sustainable for the planet and better for your health.
18. Travel to a new place as often as you can.
19. Juice more often and use the pulp to supplement your dog's food. If you don't have pets, you can add the pulp to soup stocks and even make crackers.
20. Learn to be comfortable in your own skin.
21. Imagine world peace.
22. Be more bold and adventurous.
23. Watch funny movies.
24. Give things you no longer need to others that might need them.
25. Instead of purchasing that new item, see if you can just borrow it.
26. When you are brushing your teeth, stand on one foot at a time to help your balance.
27. Plant a tree, matter of fact plant as many trees as you can. Fruit trees would be a terrific choice. Even start a tree-planting program for your community.
28. Meet all your neighbors. Love your neighbors. Help create a sense of community.
29. Call your mom. Call your dad. Keep in touch with your siblings.
30. Fill your heart with love, light and truth.
31. Learn to love and respect all sentient beings.
32. Be kind.
33. Live with integrity.
34. Be honest and speak the truth.
35. Take an online class. There are plenty of free online classes. Set up a weekly schedule of increasing your knowledge and learn a new skill. You could even learn how to write computer code and gain another income.

36. Less is more.

37. Keep it simple.

38. Don't eat anything from a box.

39. Breathe in love and breathe out peace.

40. Stretch more. Being more limber as we age is important.

41. Purchase a food dehydrator and learn about the many ways to save money, eat healthier and prepare a stash of emergency foods and rotate. Keep the temperature at 115% degrees or below to keep the vitamins and nutrients alive and bio-available.

42. Turn off the water when you are brushing your teeth. You can even save more water in the shower by getting wet, turning off the shower, soaping up and then rinsing off. Or just be more conscious and take a shorter shower.

43. Don't drive when you can walk.

44. Bring your own re-useable bags to the grocery store.

45. Recycle everything you can.

46. Use cold water instead of hot.

47. Support environmentally conscious businesses.

48. Practice common courtesy. Return phone calls, emails promptly, and if you tell someone you are going to do something, do it and follow up.

49. Buy and use recycled paper.

50. Teach your children peace.

51. Batch your errands. Look at your week and pre-plan your routes to save time and money.

52. Learn about and research products you are purchasing to ensure that the creation and production of the item does not cause harm or suffering.

53. Avoid buying rainforest products. Check clothing labels; do not purchase anything with rayon, modal, viscose or Lyocell.

54. Teach your children compassion.

55. Don't kill those bugs and spiders in your home, be kind and relocate them outside. Remember the simple law of nature that everything wants to live.

56. Avoid printing if you can. With the fabulous technologies just save the screen or take a photo and store the information electronically.

57. Make two-sided copies whenever possible.

58. Carpool to go shopping.

59. Do errands on the way home from work or school.

60. Ride your bike more.

61. Plan out your meals for the week and learn how to make them fast, simple and healthy.

62. Buy environmentally safe products.

63. Use water-based paints.

64. Limit or eliminate using disposable items.

65. Use a re-useable stainless steel water container instead of buying bottled waters or any other drinks in plastic or toxic packaging. Think ahead and prepare your own healthier libations.

66. Gift-wrap creatively and use items that you've up-cycled. Think outside the box, literally!

67. Turn off computers and unplug at night.

68. Get a clothesline and hang dry your clothes. If items like your jeans are stiff just pop into your dryer for a few minutes.

69. No need to "pre-heat" an oven.

70. If you can always back into a parking space. It's quicker to get out in case of an emergency and safer viewing for pulling out.

71. Think global and support local.

72. Buy second hand. Be sure to sweep away the energy of the previous owners.

73. Cut your sponges in half to save money.

74. Get rid of the lawn and grow an edible garden.

75. Choose matches over lighters.

76. Get rid of junk mail by calling each company and opting out.

77. Fly with an e-ticket.

78. Stop paper bank statements.

79. Learn about travel hacking to save money.

80. Pay bills online.

81. Get rid of your home phone landline. You'll save a ton of money yearly.

82. Make your own naturally brewed coffee at home and save loads of money annually instead of that coffee shop visit each morning before work. Also switch to organically-sustainable-shade-grown beans that are fair-traded.

83. Get a job telecommuting.

84. Start your own business from home. Don't let money be the motivator, let your passion dictate and fuel your dream.

85. Recycle your old cell phones. There are plenty of new grassroots organizations helping this cause.

86. Cloth diapers instead of disposable.

87. Start adding more (non-white button) mushrooms to your diet as they contain B vitamins, riboflavin, niacin, potassium, pantothenic acid, copper, selenium, essential minerals and good for you trace minerals. Look to incorporate Shitake, Reishi, Turkey Tail and Portobello mushroom varieties.

88. If you don't feel you have time to go to the gym, why not create your own personal workout at home by watching videos and doing body weight workouts. This will save you money and time. There are plenty of workout and yoga videos you can purchase and download. Learn to create discipline.

89. Drink a large glass of water with fresh squeezed lemon juice every morning when you wake up.

90. Jump rope.

91. Make new friends.

92. Meditate. Start a daily practice and make this a happy habit.

93. Make your own easy healthier salad dressings.

94. Learn about eating a more whole food plant based diet.

95. Have a "chemical free" green and clean home.

96. Read all labels and ingredients. If you aren't sure what it is, study up online.

97. With all the new technology in warm clothing there is no need to buy and wear wool. The industrialized wool practices can be inhumane and cruel. If you are purchasing a wool item be sure they are from a farm that practices humane methods of raising sheep.

98. Learn about food additives.

99. Money can be a stressor in life. Learn how to create a budget and stick to it. Re-evaluate your monthly spending. Don't use credit cards. Learn to live on less.

100. What you tell yourself everyday will either lift you up or tear you down.

101. Make your own shampoos, conditioners, body washes, lotions and potions.

102. Learn about and support the production of hemp products and share with others how it can save our planet.

103. Encourage others.

104. Start developing that skill you always wanted.

105. Do a little resistance exercise daily.

106. Replace unhealthy foods with your favorite fresh fruits and veggies. You know what's good and not good for you and your body. Treat that incredible body like a temple.

107. Surround yourself with people that make you feel good.

108. Set goals for yourself.

109. Keep it all in perspective.

110. Stand up and stretch several times each hour.

111. Tell everyone how much you love them and why.

112. Take mental health days.

113. Make an adventure jar: start a collection of places to venture to and add funds weekly.

114. Learn to cook and get back into the slow food movement.

115. Don't buy or wear fur.

116. Learn about factory farming of cattle, chickens, pigs, veal, dairy, fish and shrimp.

117. Protect your hearing and be sure to wear ear plugs when you know you will be exposed to loud noises, discos, rock concerts or motor racing events. Even using everyday equipment such as lawnmowers, power tools and personal stereos can be damaging to your eardrums.

118. Prep emergency water for your home and car. Rotate every six months. Even consider purchasing water purification tablets.

119. Grow and learn every day.

120. Stop sweating the little stuff.

121. Spend money on experiences not things.

122. Don't buy any items or clothing with down feathers.

123. Learn about animal testing and why to not support products that still test.

124. Keep a daily planner.

125. Buy e-Books.

126. Don't purchase a dishwasher. If you already have one, think about donating it. Or if you feel you really enjoy having one, don't waste as much water on pre-rinsing.

127. Rediscover your strengths and put them to positive use.

128. Stream movies instead of renting or buying the physical copies.

129. Use vinegar, lemons, salt, hydrogen peroxide and baking soda for cleaning instead of nasty chemicals.

130. Learn about using essential oils and incorporate these magical oils into your life.

131. Let go of your inhibitions.

132. Just be yourself.

133. Learn about medicinal plants and herbs.

134. When something clicks just go with it.

135. Do what makes your heart sing.

136. Pick up a fun hobby.

137. Focus on how can you make the world a better place.

138. Bring out your very secret desires.

139. Opt for comedy, romance, or documentaries over violence in choosing films to watch.

140. Take an art class.

141. Wake up knowing you are going to rock the day.

142. Be your own hero.

143. You are the C.E.O. of your life.

144. Learn to sew, knit and even crochet.

145. Create an emergency list and designate a person to be the main contact. This document could include pet info, doctors, vet, medications and blood type, phone numbers, email addresses and addresses of your family, friends and neighbors. Give to each person on the list.

146. Life doesn't have a dress code. Wear what makes you feel awesome. Stop going for trends and what's the latest style. Buy for functionality and durability. Be iconoclastic.

147. Floss and brush your teeth at least twice a day. If you can, brush after each meal. Remember to brush your tongue also to keep bacteria and plaque at a minimum.

148. Learn how to make super yummy and super healthy fruit smoothies.

149. Report and help stop animal abuse.

150. Brush your teeth with baking soda and hydrogen peroxide. Stop using toxic toothpastes.

151. Learn the art of communication.

152. Spend time with friends that make you laugh.

153. Start saving your plastic bags and start making "plarn" plastic yarn for crocheting large shopping bags, baskets and even sleeping mats for the homeless.

154. Be present.

155. Engage in active listening.

156. Grow organic wheat grass and juice it.

157. Learn about mushrooms and other fungi how they are very beneficial to the planet.

158. Try new things.

159. Practice minimalism.

160. Focus on what's in your control.

161. Take responsibility for your emotions.

162. You are writing your own life script. Make it a legend.

163. Live your life backwards from your deathbed and know you lived your life to it's fullest without fear or regrets.

164. Learn how to create multiple income revenue streams.

165. Create a gratitude jar – write down what you are grateful for during the week. At the end of the year go through them and see how magical your life really is. Take those scraps of paper and make a collage.

166. Be humble.

167. Show empathy.

168. Learn to be more patient.

169. Make more global friends.

170. Opt for glass instead of plastic.

171. Expect miracles.

172. Start facing your problems head on.

173. Be honest with yourself and others.

174. Start being your true authentic self, genuinely and proudly.

175. Support the bees and create a bee friendly environment.

176. Be acutely aware of your surroundings.

177. Don't use any pesticides.

178. Start valuing the lessons your mistakes have given you.

179. Learn a new word daily and use it throughout the day.

180. Start being more polite to yourself.

181. Start enjoying the things you already have.

182. Be happy now.

183. Believe you are ready for your next step.

184.   Forgive and move on.

185.   Always listen and trust to your inner voice and gut.

186.   Help others around you.

187.   Be sure to always protect your eyes, by wearing protective glasses or goggles when using mechanical tools or dealing with chemicals that could harm your vision.

188.   Start to really notice all the beauty around you.

189.   Make your own natural mosquito, flea, tick and bug repellents for you, your family and pets. There are many essential oils such as catnip, lemon, clove, cinnamon and neem that repel biting insects. Avoid Deet or any other toxic chemicals.

190.   Start accepting things when less than perfect.

191.   Flea comb your pets daily and avoid using toxic chemicals on them and you.

192.   Do something daily that your future self will thank you for.

193.   Start being more open about how you feel and never stuff your emotions.

194.   Learn now to make your own easy hot or cold vegetarian soups. Make big batches at a time to save money and time. Freeze half the batch for later and just reheat.

195.   Take time to learn more about cradle-to-cradle sustainable products.

196.   Be active in nurturing your relationships.

197.   Take full responsibility for your own life.

198.   Focus on positive outcomes.

199.   Notice how wealthy and healthy you are right now.

200.   Make bird feeders.

201.   Don't spend time with energy vampires.

202.   Learn to say no.

203.   Do laundry less and wash outer garments even less.

204.   Support beauty products that are not tested on animals.

205.   If you have pets be sure to have a separate sponge for cleaning their food and water bowls.

206. Don't eat anything that has a TV commercial.

207. Always soak your nuts and seeds to release the enzyme inhibitors. This helps you to maximize the goodness and nutrients that are jam-packed in these beauties. Dehydrate at 115% degrees overnight or until completely dried. If you don't have a dehydrator, you could use your oven at the very lowest temperature for 15 minutes and store in freezer when completely cooled.

208. Donate unwanted blankets to the local animal shelters.

209. Join movements doing positive things for the planet and animals.

210. When buying jewelry do not support the diamond business or other natural resources that harm the environment and supports slave and child labor. We all need to look at reinventing the wedding and engagement ring.

211. Support organic, sustainable and cruelty-free items, accessories, clothing and furniture.

212. Step outside your comfort zones.

213. Life is short and can end in an instant. Live each day to it's the fullest.

214. If you don't like something about yourself, change it.

215. Learn about fair-trade consumerism.

217. Accept that it's good to make mistakes.

218. Place a water feeder in your yard for the birds and animals.

219. Be aware of your prejudices and biases.

220. Start a free hug campaign.

221. Learn about palm oil and help others to not purchase any items that contain it.

222. Become a voice for the animals.

223. The average life span is 75 years of age. When you are 55 years old, get a huge glass jar and fill it with 1,000 marbles. Every Saturday take one out. By watching the marbles diminish you'll realize how much more life you have left.

224. Use only non-toxic products on your lawns and shrubs.

225. Take a writing class.

226. Don't waste food. It's better to buy an average amount and eat it instead of over-buying and in the end, tossing away the leftovers. If you do have leftovers get creative.
227. Just act silly.
228. Learn a water and snow sport.
229. Cuddle more.
230. Pick up your litter and others.
231. Don't let your children or pets play with wildlife.
232. Teach children to respect all living creatures.
233. Drive carefully and defensively. Like the racecar drivers, learn to scan your rearview mirror and side mirrors often. Always anticipate the need to brake quickly.
234. Don't drink alcohol excessively.
235. Make sure all the products you purchase are not GMO-Genetically Modified-Organisms.
237. Learn about sustainable-sourced fair-trade chocolate and support those companies.
238. Only buy organic fruits and vegetables.
239. Kill your television. Seriously, don't watch the plug in drug.
240. Make sure your gas tank in your car never gets below ½ or ¼ tank.
241. Keep learning with online videos and documentaries.
242. Don't stay in a job you hate.
243. Listen to how your body feels when you first meet someone.
244. Be courageous.
245. Love your family unconditionally.
267. Join a nature conservation group.
268. Connect with all your senses.
269. Join online forums helping good causes.
270. Send love, light and truth daily to all sentient beings. Expand these good wishes to the past, present and future and even to all dimensions.
271. Love your beautiful body.

272. Instead of fish oil supplements eat more flax and chia seeds.

273. Don't exploit marine wildlife for fashion, i.e., tortoise shells, coral, etc.

274. Wear faux leather instead of real leather. Many new cruelty-free companies are popping up.

275. Become an awesome eco-warrior and help educate others about joining the hippest new movement.

277. Free your heart from hatred.

278. Expect less.

279. Be a warrior not a worrier.

280. Make your home a sanctuary. Paint walls in your favorite colors, grow lots of plants, make your own fun pillows, add chimes and even think about having a small water fountain.

281. Play more often. Play as though your life depends on it.

282. Do something for someone else.

283. Minimize your exposure to wireless technology and EMF-Electro-Magnetic-Field, by using your smart-phone wisely; use your tablet on "airplane mode" when you can; purge your bedroom of any electronics; get rid of cordless phones and digital baby monitors.

284. Always look for the good in the world rather than the bad.

285. Don't pick flowers out in nature. Let them re-seed themselves. Enjoy their beauty by just admiring or taking photos.

287. Create peace in your life.

288. Stop supporting the diary industry and learn how to make nut milks. Better for the planet and way better for your body.

289. Allow yourself to be the brilliant person you are meant to be.

290. Relish great magical moments.

291. Look up often at the night sky and count the shining stars.

292. Make a list of what is truly important to you.

293. Take daily action on your goals.

294. Walk a mile in someone else's shoes.

295. You really do reap what you sow.

296. Set up an emergency kit in your home and in your car. Make a mini kit for traveling.
297. Help your child find an activity that they are passionate about.
298. For healthy hair, brush 100 times a day to stimulate new growth and keep your hair shiny.
299. Build meaningful relationships.
300. Learn about sacred geometry.
301. Teach your children about love, happiness, respect and kindness through your actions.
302. Do small, unexpected things for family and friends.
303. Start living like you only have 6 months to live.
304. Cultivate common interests with your partner.
305. Don't be afraid of monsters. Matter of fact, don't be afraid of anything. Be fearless.
306. Make trust and forgiveness your default mode.
307. Learn about an obscure scientist or doctor and what contributions they made.
308. Make your own gifts.
309. Grow your own herb garden.
310. Focus on what your partner does right not what they do wrong.
311. Learn about Fibonacci numbers and how everything in the Universe is connected.
312. Before purchasing an item think whether it's a need or a want.
313. Question everything.
314. Take the road less traveled.
315. Become a beacon of light for those in the dark.
317. Luck comes to those who believe they are lucky.
318. Success is in your DNA.
319. Support clean free energy sources. Look at ways you can incorporate solar, wind and other clean free energy sources into your home. Teach others the benefits.
320. Know that money is NOT a measure of success.

321. Follow the money and free yourself of the matrix.
322. Gain control and take your power back.
323. Learn about puppy and cat mills and why we must not support them.
324. Learn that money is a tool not a goal.
325. Let go of what others think of you.
326. Seek good mentors.
327. True love is not about finding yourself in another.
328. Self love is the best way to find real love. Remember F.L.Y. (First Love Yourself)
329. Throw eco-friendly parties.
330. Take more naps.
331. To get love, you must give love.
332. Don't read everything you believe in and don't believe everything you read.
333. Learn about a spiritual guru and their journey to self-enlightenment.
334. Listen to your favorite music.
335. Dance and shake your groove thing more often.
337. Learn to compost your food scraps and how this can help nourish your garden and planet.
338. Practice water wise landscaping. Learn about plants and shrubs that thrive on less water.
339. Voluntourism – helping others while on vacation.
340. Don't drink alcohol and drive.
341. Follow your dreams.
342. Stop pretending you are someone else.
343. Don't burn bridges; however if you need to, know you can swim.
344. Read labels and don't consume anything artificial.
345. Be fearless and live with courage.
346. Do everything with love.
347. Don't take your family and friends for granted. As a matter of fact, don't take anything for granted.

348. Stand up for yourself and others.
349. Set up your life like a vacation.
350. Smile and say hello to everyone you walk past.
351. Stop following commands and instead ask why.
352. What one thing can you do today to help make another life better.
353. Carpe the hell out of this Diem.
364. Carpe the hell out of this Noctum.
365. Change one tiny bad habit.
366. Get active and start exercising. Not just for your body, but for your brain and wellbeing.
367. Kill negative thoughts.
368. Put effort into looking and feeling your best.
369. Celebrate your achievements.
370. Practice proficiency.
371. Learn to whistle and/or always carry a whistle with you.
372. Take the stress out of traveling and just pack simply in a backpack.
373. Get more plants for your living space. There are terrific choices for plants that create more oxygen and help to clean the air of toxins.
374. Action speaks louder than words so notice what you are saying and your actions.
375. Have faith that things will always work out.
377. Hope for a better world today.
378. Eat more raw garlic to kill unwanted parasites.
379. Look for more ways to reduce your impact on the planet.
380. With companies your money talks so think about your purchasing power. Remember, if there isn't a market for an item the company will most likely stop producing it.
381. Watch documentary films that are for the good of the planet.
382. Organize a get together with all your neighbors and create a community.
383. Take pride in where you live.
384. Research charities and join or donate to help their causes.

385. Look for more ways to help the environment.

386. Go through your clothes, shoes and accessories more often and donate what you are not wearing.

387. Encourage and vote for legislation that protects animals and their welfare.

388. Just be nice.

389. Tutor at your local grade school.

390. Don't waste food. Only take what you can eat. Bring a container when eating out.

391. Protect and speak up for the weak.

392. Help the elderly with their groceries or even shop for them.

393. Assist your neighbors with their yard work.

394. Turn off lights in rooms you are not using.

395. Hug at least 11 times a day for good health and wellness.

396. Add papaya and the seeds to your smoothies to help kill parasites.

397. Conserve more water at home, check for leaks and don't over water your yard.

398. Shatter your limits.

399. Contact your local water representative and speak up about your views on keeping water chemical free.

400. Volunteer to keep beaches and riverbanks clean.

401. Shut off electrical equipment and even unplug when not in use.

402. Take a different route instead of always going the same direction.

403. Plant more trees to shade your home.

404. Drive less. Better yet live without a car. Donate your car. Take public transportation.

405. Become an air pollution activist.

406. Fly less.

407. Maintain and repair durable products instead of buying new ones.

408. Reuse items like paper, envelopes, folders and paper clips.

409. Mend clothes instead of buying new ones. Use fun expressive sewing patches.

410. Raise awareness on the environmental damage from clear cutting and deforestation.
411. Make your property a haven for wildlife.
412. Work to protect animal habitat.
413. Educate yourself and others to promote environmentally responsible mining.
414. Plant shrubs and trees that attract wildlife.
415. Don't use any chemical pesticides and learn about other natural companion planting to reduce unwanted pests.
416. Use outdoor solar powered lights.
417. Install a shower water recycler and learn about re-using grey water.
418. Let all creatures live, just relocate them away from your home and back into nature.
419. Be grateful for your hardships for they have taught you many lessons.
420. Use humane traps and relocate the animal.
421. Use a manual lawnmower instead of a gas powered one.
422. Put on a sweater instead of turning on the heat.
423. Don't buy products with a lot of packaging.
424. Get rid of your microwave oven.
425. Take a shower instead of a bath, a bath uses 36 gallons of water vs. 3-5 gallons.
426. When watering your yard, water early in the AM or later PM so it doesn't evaporate as quickly.
427. Don't purchase or use any kind of disposable products.
428. Turn down your water heater temperature.
429. Use half the amount of household products.
430. Don't make assumptions. Find the courage to ask questions and to express what you really want.
431. Turn off your car engine; it's more fuel-efficient than running for more than 45 seconds.
432. Use a recycled bath mat to keep from slipping in the shower or tub.

433. Learn how to use fresh herbs to create tastier meals and backing off from adding too much salt.

434. Explore the use of natural sweeteners like the Stevia plant.

435. Don't reward yourself with food.

436. Teach others to not support wars and why wars must be stopped to save our planet.

437. Stay away from white sugar and white bread.

438. Ride your bike instead of driving to work or for errands.

439. Use banana peels for shining shoes. Matter of fact there are many uses for banana peels such as skin irritations, bug bites, silverware shiner, fertilizer, and teeth whitener.

440. Eat more healthy spices.

441. Stop wallowing in self-pity.

442. Think of the very worst that can happen then work on positive thoughts to prevent them.

443. Stop drinking diet sodas or any artificial chemicals. Stop and think about what you are consuming and ask yourself is this health promoting or health hurting. Be smarter than the advertisement and propaganda.

444. Research childhood and pet vaccinations and what's in them.

445. Learn about your possible food and allergy sensitivities. Learn about muscle testing.

447. Our bodies need a ton of natural goodness. Start your day off with a spinach or chard green smoothie. Add bananas, papaya, pineapple, spirulina, flax or chia seeds and Aloe Vera.

448. Avoid fluoride.

449. Learn more about heavy metal toxicity and how you can prevent this.

450. Have your mercury fillings removed.

451. Be mindful of your breath and take deep belly breaths.

452. Make sure you love your comfortable bedroom. Create a dream haven by decorating inexpensively with fun things you just simply love. Make sure your bedroom is in complete darkness at night for better sound sleeping.
453. Learn the essential basic safety knots for tying ropes.
454. Devote part of your day to reducing stress in your life.
455. Avoid eating too much sugar, salt, and saturated fats.
456. Get at least 30 minutes of moderate to intense exercise every day.
457. Boost your immune system with more raw ginger in your diet.
458. Get up and stretch more during the day.
459. Learn about Chinese medicine and your body's acupressure and meridian points.
460. Try to get into a rhythm of going to bed the same time every night.
461. Eat plenty of fruits, vegetables and whole grains.
462. Take a self-defense class.
463. Don't harbor negative thoughts, work it out or just forgive and forget.
464. Keep your skin healthy by moisturizing with coconut oil through out the day.
465. Give compliments.
466. Set up a no phone zone in your home, especially during meals.
467. Go out and have some fun with friends.
468. Really take an honest look at your life and evaluate all the stressors and work to remove anything that stresses you out.
469. Don't hunch, sit and stand up straight.
470. Soak your fruits and veggies in a bath wash of 1 to 4 ratio of vinegar and water for at least 20 minutes and rinse well.
471. Stay clear away from products that contain nitrates, such as processed meats.
472. Drink a green smoothie before you go out to a holiday party to help curb your appetite and help you to not over-indulge.
473. Enroll in a martial arts class.

474. Teach yourself how to have a photographic memory. Practice remembering phone numbers, license plates, and even start to memorize street names and locations.

475. Learn about diseases and how they are caused and prevented.

477. If you are taking medication, take a look at what is causing the symptoms and is this treatable with alternative behaviors and lifestyle changes.

478. Install a smoke detector.

479. Know thyself.

480. Avoid fluorescent lighting.

481. Sleep naked.

482. Build more muscle, because you'll feel and look sexier and it's important to keep those muscles toned especially as we age.

483. Learn more than is expected, knowledge is power.

484. Eat more pumpkin seeds. Traditionally used to kill parasites and a terrific source of zinc, vitamins K, E and B, magnesium, and improves bladder function.

485. Make love more often.

486. Every time you look in the mirror tell yourself how much you love yourself.

487. Schedule "nothing" time on your calendar.

488. Choose an upbeat personal theme song to motivate yourself.

489. Plant more plants that attract more butterflies and birds to your garden.

490. Make and sell re-cycled and up-cycled jewelry.

491. Make your own natural teeth whitener with a strawberry and baking soda mashed together.

492. To keep your children safer, create a password that only you and your children know just in case you have to send a friend to pick up your children.

493. Before you take a trip or vacation, scan all your documents i.e., travel itinerary; hotel stay info; conference info; passports, etc. and email it to yourself, friends and family just in case of an emergency.

494. Get rid of friends that are very negative and put you down.

495. Clean out your kitchen drawers and cabinets and donate what you don't use.

496. Go through your storage and garage and get rid of all toxic chemicals safely.

497. Buy energy efficient appliances.

498. Do all ironing at one time and be sure to turn off and unplug your iron.

499. Use organic coconut oil as a sexual lubricant instead of toxic chemicals.

500. Write companies urging them to use paper rather than plastics and Styrofoam.

501. Support people doing great work for the good of the order.

502. Install water-efficient showerheads and faucets.

503. Use non-aluminum pots and pans.

504. Avoid any soaps with sodium laurel sulfate.

505. If you have babies and children keep them away from any products containing BPA, anti-bacterial wipes, hand sanitizers, phylates, synthetic bedding and clothing ingredients, flame retardant clothing, mineral oil, plastic toys, diapers, toxic shampoos and conditioners and all toxic bathing and grooming products.

506. Cook with quick heating, copper-bottom pans to conserve energy.

507. Don't buy fire extinguishers containing halon.

508. Avoid skin care products containing parabens. Parabens are endocrine disruptors, developmental and reproductive toxicity, and may cause allergies and immunotoxicity.

509. Build a garden green house. You can even use re-cycled materials.

510. Start a vertical wall garden. Indoor and out. Learn to maximize gardening space.

511. Make your own easy and healthy veggie and chip dips.

512. Drink more Kombucha. This amazing elixir detoxifies the body, great for joint care, aids digestion and gut health and a terrific immune booster. Even learn about making your own and give the

new Kombucha scoby babies as gifts to your family and friends and teach them how to make this healthy drink.

513. Take off your shoes more and step into the dirt to get grounded.

514. If you don't know how to swim, taking swimming lessons.

515. Do more things you are afraid of to build self-confidence.

516. Learn to trim your own hair. Opt for an easy natural hairstyle that also uses fewer products.

517. Stop dying your hair with nasty toxic chemicals. Embrace your own natural beauty and love your curly or straight hair and whatever natural color you have.

518. Write thank you notes and mail them. Get crafty and make your own note cards with fun scraps and up cycling what you have already.

519. Engage in active listening and learn to pause before responding.

520. Celebrate every day like it's your birthday.

521. Purchase some good quality hanker-chiefs and use those instead of purchasing tissues. It produces less waste, saves resources and will save you money. Even think of giving them as gifts.

522. Stay away from propylene glycol common in shampoos, soaps, baby wipes and lotions.

523. Don't purchase anything with phthalates in it – common in fragrances and plastics.

524. Stop right now and think about all the little things you are grateful for.

525. What are some terrific qualities you like in other people and think about how you can add those to your character.

526. Create buddy systems for doing fun events.

527. Before putting anything into the garbage think of ways to reuse it. Remember, there is no such thing as throwing something away. Get crafty and find all the many ways to up cycle.

528. Watch out for products that say "derived from coconut" the manufacturer could be hiding the nasty chemicals Cocamide DEA/Lauramide DEA, which are harmful to your immune system.

529. Purchase from only earth friendly companies that have little or no carbon footprint.

530. One of the scariest chemicals added to cosmetics is Diazolidinyl Urea, which acts as a Formaldehyde releaser and is an antimicrobial preservative. It's one of the highest toxic class ingredients that could cause cancer.

531. Sorry folks, reconsider painting your nails. Nails are living tissue and need to breath.

532. Eat less meat. Meat-based diets require more land, water and energy to sustain. One hamburger patty takes over 600 gallons of water to produce.

533. Learn about the Amazon and how they function as our earth's lungs. Join forces with others to help stop the deforestation of this vital region of the planet.

534. Stay away from Butyl Acetate, which is commonly found in fingernail products.

535. Think and create.

536. Support truthful journalism and news. Be skeptical of the mainstream media, be a critical thinker.

537. Commune with nature. Aim to get at least sometime outside every single day.

538. Be body conscious. Appreciate the little sings and signals from your body, when it tells you it's tired, it's joyful, in need of love or getting sick.

539. Learn to just let go. The Universe is in charge, just go with the flow.

540. The secret of good health is to live fully in the now.

541. Don't believe everything you are told to believe.

542. Control your mind or it will control you, listen to your inner knowing.

543. Knowing yourself is true enlightenment.

544. Don't buy lipstick, moisturizers or deodorant with Butylated Hdroxytoluene BHT.

545. Replace jealousy with admiration.

546. Doubt separates while trust unites.

547. Give up labels and judging.

548. Choose your friends wisely.

549. Avoid Ethyl Acetate, which is a solvent in oil-based lacquers and enamels.

550. Let go of attachments.

551. You loose what you cling, to so let things be free.

552. Learn and practice Qi Gong.

553. Have the courage to express your feelings.

554. Allow yourself to experience bliss, joy and love daily.

555. Work at staying in touch with good friends no matter if they are near or far.

556. Don't buy anything with Toluene in it. It is a very toxic chemical and can harm unborn children.

557. Always stay true to yourself and do what you want in life not what others expect of you.

558. Learn and practice Tai Chi.

559. If you feel like crying you should cry. The beauty of life is to feel its ups and downs.

560. Every night before falling asleep think about all the wonderful and magical things that happened that day and be grateful.

561. Give your dogs a raw garlic clove in their food at least several times a week to keep parasites away. Simply grate finely and sprinkle on their meal.

562. Feed your cat a raw egg several times a week. Think what cats would be eating out in the wild.

563. Take a beekeeping class and become a beekeeper if you have space and or encourage your neighbors to have a community garden with beekeeping to help with the declining bee population and help the pollination process.

564. Raise chickens and or ducks to help with your permaculture garden.

565.   Avoid products containing Petrolatum aka Mineral Oil, Paraffin, or Vaseline.

566.   Let the dandelions in your garden grow and use the greens in your salads or juice.

567.   You don't need to wash your hair everyday. Get creative and play with different hairstyles. Slightly dirty hair actually keeps a better curl and up do's.

568.   Drink more organic green teas. Helps to lower cholesterol, prevents cavities, protects against heart disease, speeds metabolism, full of antioxidants, supports digestion and aids in healthy skin.

569.   Tame tension headaches by rubbing peppermint oil, Tiger Balm, or white flower oil into your temples. All three remedies contain menthol, which has analgesic properties.

570.   To stay sharp, try smelling fresh rosemary or inhaling the scent of rosemary essential oil before a test or meeting.

571.   Cultivate good gut flora by eating sauerkraut and other types of fermented foods. Learn how simple and easy it is to make your own, for you, your family and friends.

573.   Eat potassium rich bananas, cantaloupe and oranges.

574.   Go get a massage. Incorporate massages into your wellness lifestyle.

575.   Make sure to eat more avocados. An awesome super food chock full of good oils that your body and brain needs. Don't forget to save the seeds to help them grow into trees and give as gifts or plant in your garden. If you don't live in a warmer climate avocado plants make terrific indoor plants.

576.   Grow Echinacea, dandelions, mint, spearmint, peppermint and chamomile in your garden and make your own teas.

577.   Invest and use a Neti Pot for gentle sinus flushing. A terrific habit, especially during allergy or cold season.

578.   For heel and arch pain (plantar fasciistis), roll your feet on a tennis ball.

579. Don't wear high heels often. If you do, choose to wear them when you know you'll be sitting more than standing, as they are very hard on your back and skeletal system. Ladies be sure to not wear them especially when you are on your monthly period, this can actually cause more menstrual cramping due to the pressure on your lower back. If you are pregnant be sure to only wear lower or flat heals for the same reasons because this tilts your pelvis forward which increases the curve in your back, which can create painful discomfort for you and the baby.

580. Learn about acupressure and other self-healing techniques.

581. Wash your hands often using plain soap and water.

582. Fennel seeds are considered a carminative, a substance that helps relieve gas.
      Chew and then swallow about half a teaspoon of the seeds after meals.

583. Research suggests that pineapple juice may be more effective than cough syrup. Take 2 teaspoons at bedtime.

584. Start purchasing chia seeds and add them to your diet. They are packed full of potassium, iron, fiber, calcium, selenium, omega-3's, magnesium, protein, phosphorus, foliate, lignans and antioxidants.

585. Purchase a good cross-shredder for discarding your receipts, old bills and confidential documents. Also consider saving all your paper to make paper-mache projects.

586. Wear super comfy flat shoes.

587. Stock your medicine cabinet with a bottle of Tea Tree Oil. It helps stop bug bites from itching, clears sinuses, terrific insect repellent, bathroom cleaner, treats cuts and bruises, anti-fungal and cleans off mold and mildew. Practice extreme caution if you own cats or dogs. Tea Tree Oil can kill cats and it's extremely toxic to dogs. Read pet grooming labels to be sure this isn't one of the ingredients.

588. Naturally improve your glorious hair with Primrose Oil aka Gamma-linolenic-acid. Other great essential oils to massage into your scalp are lemongrass, lavender, rosemary, geranium, and tea tree.

589. Connect with friends that make you smile, laugh and giggle.

590. Learn about food combining and how to help your digestive system be more efficient.

591. Lay with your legs vertical up the wall. This exercise encourages drainage of the blood and lymphatic fluid from your feet and legs into the abdomen, where these fluids can be more easily cleansed and it nourishes the digestive organs and helps with circulatory issues.

592. Stop purchasing paper napkins and use cloth napkins.

593. For greasy pots and pans scour with salt or baking soda.

594. Always opt for glass containers versus plastic for storage and daily use.

595. Unclog your sink naturally. As is, baking soda won't necessarily clear a pathway. It first needs to change its chemical composition. Boiling water converts baking soda into sodium carbonate a more effective drain cleaner. Pour 1 cup of baking soda down the drain, followed by 3 cups of boiling water and let science take over. This method is cleaner and safer then commercial products.

596. Start chilling your water if you like it cold. Keep a pitcher of water in the frig instead of running your tap until it runs cold. Kitchen faucets flow at an average rate of more than a gallon per minute.

597. Try not to buy or use aluminum foil. If you do, always recycle it.

598. Fill up your freezer. When a freezer is full it uses less energy.

599. Try to have more "no-cook meals" to save the oven and the planet.

600. Make your own laundry detergent by using vinegar and baking soda.

601. Try not to purchase clothes that need to be dry-cleaned.

602. For a greener bedroom only purchase organic cotton bedding and bath towels.

603. If you need to paint your house buy eco-paints that have very low levels of VOC's aka volatile-organic-compounds.

604. Open more windows instead of using the air-conditioner, and use fans strategically.

605. Use easy natural stain removers such as cornstarch, white vinegar, lemon juice and or even hydrogen peroxide. Pre-soak with a bit of water before laundering.

606. Get creative and buy recycled clothing and create your own look.

607. Support sustainable goods from indigenous people from other countries going to good causes. Make sure they aren't exploiting limited resources or harming the environment.

608. Non-toxic tub scrub using 1-teaspoon liquid soap, essential oils such as tea tree, lavender, eucalyptus, rosemary or peppermint and 1 cup of baking soda. Just enough water to form a paste and use it with a sponge or brush.

609. Avoid PVC shower curtains. Purchase non-vinyl curtains instead. Be sure to clean often keeping it mold free.

610. Buy toilet paper that has been recycled from other paper products.

611. Make your own air fresheners by using just water and a few drops of your favorite essential oils. Place in a spritzing bottle.

612. For fun cosmetic face masks you can use bananas, grapefruits, avocados, papayas, and essential oils.

613. Save money and make your own spice blends. This is also much healthier since most store bought spice blends have MSG, additives and non-caking agents. Make your own taco and chili blends, Italian seasoning mix, Asian 5-spice blend, pumpkin pie spice, Caribbean Jerk seasoning and just get creative. Even consider drying onion and garlic and grind to a powder to add to the spice mixes. Purchase a coffee grinder to use just for your herbs and spices.

614. Save a ton of money on beauty products. Make your own organic beauty remedies by just visiting your kitchen. You can make salt or sugar scrubs, bath salts and fizzies. DIY stuff can be great gifts especially during the holidays.

615. Opt for bamboo fiber for flooring and furniture since it's one of the fastest growing woody plants on earth.

616. During the winter, open your shades to take advantage of the warmth from the sun.

617.   If you live in a cold area of the world, opt for insulating drapes to preserve warmth.

618.   Most candles are made of paraffin, a petroleum derivative; consider burning only beeswax and soy-based candles with cotton wicks. Be especially careful if you have birds and pets.

619.   Don't use fake fireplace logs that are full of petroleum and paraffin waxes, which are bad for your health and the environment.

620.   When choosing new furniture make sure it's eco-friendly. Make sure the company uses sustainable grown woods, natural fibers and recycled glass to produce their goods.

621.   Install better energy efficient windows.

622.   Always unplug electronics when not in use.

623.   Buy in bulk if you use a certain product or food more often.

624.   When traveling be sure to check the bed for bedbugs. If your room has bedbugs change rooms. When you travel back home, be sure to wash all clothing, even the ones you did not wear and if you can wash your luggage or vacuum.

625.   Donate old electronics.

626.   Apply weather stripping on your doors.

627.   Leave clippings and yard trimmings in your compost pile, bin, or in your yard to nourish the soil and help keep moisture from evaporating.

628.   Choose safer antifreeze for your car.

629.   Use eco-friendly car-wash-water-less products that are plant based cleaners that do not require using water.

630.   Get a green thumb and learn all about growing the best healthy edible plants and wild weeds.

631.   Do away with a green lawn and grow more veggies and even plant spreading thyme, which will attract more bees and smell heavenly.

632.   Build an edible arbor and grow beans and blooming clematis. Learn more about companion planting and permaculture.

633.   Be 100% independent.

634.   For potted plants use drip irrigators.

635. Watch more films and documentaries for action, and get inspired.

636. Make a bucket list of things you want to do before you die.

637. You are what you eat so it's best to choose wisely.

639. Use white vinegar to clean your windows.

640. Making your own perfumes are simple, safer for you, and the environment. All you need is a spray bottle, an almond oil base and a few drops of your favorite essential oils.

641. Don't use any toxic paints or art supplies, especially with children.

642. Whenever your electronics, such as your laptop, cell phones or tablets get to 100% fully charged, unplug and let drain all the way back down below 10% before recharging.

643. Imagine what your perfect day looks like and live it.

644. Eat more sage to help boost your memory.

645. Stay on top of groundbreaking news that supports clean free energy. Share these articles and help get this info out virally.

646. Don't buy anything with Triethanolamine aka TEA in it. This can be shaving foams, skin lotions, eye gels, moisturizers and shampoos.

647. When a product is labeled "anti-bacterial" stay away from it. This toxic chemical, Triclosan is linked to numerous liver and inhalation toxicity and causes disrupted thyroid functions. This also ends up in our water supply and it is very toxic to aquatic life.

648. Turmeric is a magical root and spice, make sure you learn more about it and eat it more often during the week.

649. Get your Omega-3 awesome fatty acids from eating more walnuts.

650. If you are craving chocolate you could also be magnesium deficient. Make your own easy magnesium oil spray by purchasing magnesium chloride flakes and distilled water. Boil the distilled water and pour over the flakes, let cool then put into a spray bottle. Spray daily on chest and underarms.

651. Renew some of your old clothes with natural dyes such as coffee, teas, plants or flowers. Be creative and use beets, plums, carrots,

grape juice, lemons and red cabbage. You can use a salt or vinegar to fix the dye and cause the dye adhere to your fabric.

652. Strike a balance between saving and experiencing.

653. Buy Epsom salts and do a nice bath soak. It's a safe and effective way to increase the body's levels of both magnesium and sulfate. Soaking in Epsom salts also help to soothe aching muscles and remove toxins from the body.

654. Make sure to eat more beets because it's a super food. Chock full of iron, magnesium, calcium, phosphorus and a terrific energy and immunity booster. Juicing weekly will rock your body.

655. The effort it takes to supremely organize your paperwork is always worth it.

656. Join the barefoot running and walking revolution. Start slowly on soft surfaces.

657. You need to start being brutally honest with yourself.

658. Listen to how you feel.

659. Plan your retirement and beyond.

660. Learn to say hello, please and thank you in every language.

661. Try new foods.

662. Place fresh herbs and leafy greens in a jar or vase of water and place in frig for longer lasting produce.

663. Learn about edible flowers and add those to your salads.

664. Just say no to putting all of your produce in plastic bags. Bring your own smaller organic cotton re-useable bags or recycle the ones from previous shopping.

665. Buy from bulk bins as often as possible.

666. Return containers for berries, cherry tomatoes, etc. to the farmers markets to be reused.

667. Store potatoes with apples to keep the potatoes from sprouting.

668. Buy fresh bread that comes in either paper bags or no bags.

669. Avoid purchasing frozen foods. Usually expensive and contain too much sodium.

670. Carry reusable utensils and glass drinking straws in your purse, backpack and car.

671. Consider drying your herbs to make them last longer. Just tie with a string and store upside down until dried.

672. Make onions last up to 8 months by storing them in old clean panty hose, tying them in knots in between and hang from the ceiling.

673. Carry a stainless steel travel mug and water bottle at all times for drinks around town and the world.

674. Keep tomatoes at room temperature and away from sunlight to last longer.

675. Make your own nut butters. Simply roast the nuts on a cookie sheet at 150-170 degrees Fahrenheit until lightly browned. Put the roasted nuts into a food processor and add 2-3 tablespoons of olive oil and salt to taste. Store in glass jars in the refrigerator.

676. Try not to pack your frig as the cooler air needs to keep circulating to help preserve your food longer.

677. Store grains and nuts in freezer to last longer.

678. Find something beautiful and appreciate it.

679. Stop gossiping.

680. Only speak highly of your fellow Earth mates. Focus on the good.

681. Keep your fridge clean. Leftover residue or mold spores can increase the spoilage of all your food in the fridge. Make it a habit to do a thorough cleaning once a month.

682. Time heals most everything.

683. Everything you think you know for sure will probably change.

684. Make your own organic apple cider vinegar. This magical vinegar can help with diabetes, joint pain, grout, manage blood sugar levels, and aid to help you loose weight.

685. Invest in a good quality blender like the Vitamix.

686. Make super healthy and fun kid-friendly lunches and snacks. Great online resources for ideas and simple back to basic recipes to keep your children strong, growing and super healthy. Those little

magical bodies need more enzymes, nutrients and natural whole plant based goodness for brain and body development.

687. Eat more organic carrots or juice them more frequently.

688. Learn about cardiovascular diseases and how to prevent them.

689. Make a healthier version of ice cream with coconut milk.

690. Sweep more often and keep dust mites down.

691. For dusting around the house just use a towel and water.

692. Learn to sprout and add to your salads daily.

693. Change your online passwords often and making them difficult with caps and numbers. Make a note on your monthly planner or at least quarterly.

694. Stay organized with a monthly planner.

695. Save rainwater.

696. Release mediocrity.

697. Aim for genius.

698. Help to educate others of what you are learning to save the planet.

699. Carpool with friends to go shopping.

700. Share awesome vegan/vegetarian recipes with friends, family and get out virally with social media.

701. Don't use ATM machines and just plan on doing your banking once a month.

702. For holiday decorations, get creative and recycle what you already own and use the same decorations annually. There are a zillion things you can use, plastic bottles, paint, glitter, cardboard, leaves and branches from nature, etc.

703. Aspire to not have more but to be more.

704. Invest in a professional kitchen knife and knife sharpener.

705. You already know what's wrong and right, always do the right thing.

706. Learn more about home schooling and why it might be a better choice for your children.

707. When you plan to go to the store, call your neighbor and see what they might need.

708. Let everyone see the real, quirky, wacky, weird and flawed person that you are.

709. Learn to make your own healthier pet food.

710. Use a bamboo cutting board because it's anti-microbial.

711. Clean your kitchen sponges by dowsing it in rubbing alcohol or hydrogen peroxide several times a week.

712. Learn to appreciate other countries culinary cuisine by jumping online and finding some yummy recipes using the different herbs and spices of that country.

713. Keep re-using those plastic bags by gently washing with warm soapy water and turn inside out to dry.

714. If you are using plastic wrap, keep and reuse.

715. Next time you attend a potluck, instead of using plastic wrap, by two glass bowls and place your goodies in one dish and place the other dish on top and then wrap the two bowls together with a nice large pretty dish towel. Called Furoshiki-Style which comes from Japan.

716. Make your own healthy energy bars with peanut butter, figs, dates, nuts and seeds.

717. Instead of purchasing tea already in those little chemical-laden bags, just boil water and place herbs in your cup and pour the hot water over the herbs and let steep and add a few Stevia leaves for sweetener.

718. Purchase a good sturdy stainless steel pressure cooker.

719. Cook your own beans in your new pressure cooker. Find a few yummy easy bean and vegetable soup recipes to keep you healthy during the week.

720. Find easy recipes for healthy soups and easy dishes that will last you a week in the fridge or freezer. Just re-heat.

721. Clear your clutter and get organized.

722. Don't expect people to read your mind. Work at communicating with respect for each other and if you can remember to do it with love.

723. Envy blinds us to opportunities in our own life. Work on why you might have become envious, be happy for others and move on to how you can better yourself.

724. What you give is what you get in life.

725. Sometimes action is often better than no action.

726. Worry is a waste of time.

727. Seek to live authentically.

728. Where there is true love, there is no ego.

729. Cut ½ an onion and keep it on your kitchen counter to absorb airborne bacteria.

730. Deter snails and slugs in your garden by crunching up eggshells and placing them at the base of the plants.

731. Make your own chemical free and natural face powder with a cornstarch base, add a little of cinnamon, nutmeg, cocoa powder or green clay for tint.

732. Stop using toxic under-arm deodorant. It clogs those pores that need to breath and your body needs to get rid of toxins. It's healthy to sweat. If you are stinky you need to look at what you are eating. A body with a clean diet with a lot of water isn't smelly. You can make your own by just mixing a little baking soda and coconut oil. If you like add some essential oils.

733. Wherever you are, be there totally.

734. Don't take life so seriously.

735. When you complain, you make yourself a victim.

736. Give up defining yourself and others.

737. Letting go takes a lot of strength and courage.

738. Whatever you fight you strengthen, or what you resist, persists.

739. Think of more ways you can be more adventurous.

740. To remove eye-make-up just use a tissue with some olive oil or coconut oil.

741. Switch from aerosol cans to pump sprays.

742. Don't make mountains out of molehills.

743. Work on having a stress-free environment at work by listening to your favorite music or audio book and keep conversations with co-workers more positive and upbeat. If you are really stressed out, change jobs.

744. Start a gratitude journal and write in it daily. Lift your spirits by reading it often.

745. Be sure to let your children know that happiness is a choice not something that you search for like your car-keys.

746. Never feel like you have to prove your self worth to anyone, once you start to feel this way just walk away from the circumstance.

747. After you floss, just wash, rinse in alcohol or hydrogen peroxide and dry the floss thread to keep re-using. Think about the landfills filling up with the floss containers and floss. Let's reduce and re-use.

748. Chew your food completely and enjoy each savory bite. Quit rushing through your meals and stay in the present moment.

749. Avoid keeping your refrigerator or freezer too cold. A good temp for keeping food fresh in the frig is 38 degrees Fahrenheit and for freezers it is 5 degrees Fahrenheit.

750. Invest in rechargeable batteries and a re-charger.

751. Always remember that people aren't against you; they are for themselves.

752. You learn a lot more from failure than you do from success. Don't let it stop you, because failure builds character.

753. Everyone you meet is afraid of something, loves something, and has lost something.

754. Remember the future is created by what you do today not by what you do tomorrow.

755. Always believe you can.

756. If you ever find yourself in the wrong story or setting, just get up and leave.

757. The less you respond to negative people, the more peaceful your life will become.

758. It's ok to take a step back and admit you're being ridiculous.

759. Take responsibility to find beauty in the ugliest of days.

760. Keep your head up and your heart strong.

761. Have fun working at being an original and not a copy.

762. Learn to detect bullshit early on and quickly move away from it.

763. Don't let yesterday take up too much of today.

764. Do it now. Later might not ever come.

765. Popeye was right so eat plenty of spinach. Of course, always choose organic.

766. Purchase a good sturdy mini trampoline and jump on it daily.

767. Don't feed wild animals processed foods, such as white bread to ducks. Think about what you are feeding them. If it's not good for you, it's not good for animals.

768. Time to take full responsibility for your own health, your life and your knowledge.

769. Drink more organically grown green tea. Green teas are chock full of amazing goodness.

770. Every day do something little that your future self will thank you for.

771. Try the Pomodoro Technique, choose a task set your timer for 20 minutes to accomplish your goal.

772. If you really want to accomplish some goals, get a huge calendar for the year, stick it up on your wall and start setting those daily goals and mark them off as completed.

773. Put organic celery on your grocery list and make sure to eat and juice it weekly.

774. Snack on almonds for a terrific source of calcium and other terrific nutrients that feed your body and help curb your appetite.

775. For a more nurturing relationship always remember these 3 things: Attention, Affection, and Appreciation.

776. Avoid supporting specific pet breeds or shopping at a pet store. Adopt from the shelters.

777. Always spay and neuter your pets and encourage others to do the same.

778. Count to ten when you are angry.

779. Shed light on the dark evils.

780. Never text and drive. If you can also avoid being on your cell phone while you drive, the better.

781. Don't snack when you aren't hungry.

782. Be the light to help others see.

783. Always kiss each other good night.

784. Don't let past experiences make you bitter, let it make you better.

785. Collect moments not things.

786. Start off your healthy morning with organic berries and fresh fruits daily. Learn how to make yummy and nutritious fruit smoothies.

787. Be sure to eat plenty of super foods such as cruciferous vegetables, like broccoli, cauliflower, Brussels sprouts, arugula, bok choy, collard greens, radishes, kale, kohlrabi, land cress, mustard greens, rutabaga, turnips and watercress.

788. Start saving all your glass jars, glass bottles and re-use them for food storage; juicing; spices; herbs; candles; gifts containers; and children's crafts.

789. Work to be civil and polite in your conversations.

790. You are the product of your thoughts, keep choosing the positive ones.

791. Be polite and start turning off your phone when you are with friends and family.

792. Another terrific grain to start adding in your weekly diet is Quinoa, plenty of magnesium, iron, protein, phosphorus and fiber.

793. Become your biggest cheerleader and learn to push yourself in the right direction.

794. Start soaking and sprouting your own organic lentil seeds and add those to your big whopping green salads for more iron, heart health, energy, happy digestion and stabilizes blood sugar levels.

795. Never be afraid of letting go of the good to be great.

796. To deter ants from coming into your home, find their entry and simply spray with white vinegar or sprinkle cinnamon by their incoming trail.

797. Just a little reminder that you must be a friend, to find a friend.

798. Relinquish your need for approval.

799. Shed the burden of judgment.

800. No one can ruin your day without your permission.

801. Freeze an organic lemon and whenever you prepare a dish, simply take out the lemon and grate a little magic zest to brighten up the flavor and add a bit more nutrition.

802. When harvesting from your organic garden, learn how to save your seeds properly.

803. People can be jerks sometimes or they can come off as mean spirited. However, you should listen to what they're saying and not how they are saying it. There is a reason and learning how to be patient with yourself and taking the time to understand the experience, will help you grow.

804. Criticism is so essential for personal growth. Even ask for honest feedback and thank your colleagues and friends.

805. Networking is a key component to attracting more opportunities and career advancement.
    True networking is about building meaningful connections by engaging in actual conversations.

806. Share your knowledge. Have fun sharing what you've learned to help others. We are here on this planet now to assist and care for each other, the animals and environment.

807. Don't be afraid to ask for help.

808. There are tons of fun and free things you can do with your family and friends. Get creative and host a potluck, movie night, picnic, DIY craft parties, host a workshop to teach others about up cycling, play board games, volunteer together, start a book club, go camping, or even organize a scavenger hunt.

809. Plan a weekly get together for a fun jam session to sing, dance and play some music.

810. No worries if you don't have a set of drums, jump online and watch videos on how to do some exciting body percussion. It's great fun and super for improving your coordination skills.

811. Gain a sense of freedom and confidence by taking a trip by yourself.

812. Get off any social networking site entirely or place a limit using a timer and regain control of your time. Practice discipline online.

813. Be in relationships that bring out the best in each other and not the worst in each other.

814. One of the happiest moments in life is when you find the courage to let go of what you cannot change.

815. Everyone is important.

816. Never let anyone dull your sparkle.

817. Learn survival skills. Learn how to start a fire. Learn ways to be self-sufficient.

818. If you have stacks of old magazines, why not turn them into creative art or something useful. Check out all the DIY crafts for magazines and newspapers. Why not learn Origami and make your own creative gift containers.

819. Unless you puke, faint or die, keep going.

820. Your health is everything. It is the foundation from which all else is created.

821. Eating more organic apples during the day does keep the doctor away.

822. Buy that big watermelon weekly and cut it up and blend it up and add a little bit of lemon juice and pour it into a large glass jar and place in frig. You can even add some basil or mint leaves for a more fun flavor. Watermelon is jam packed full of terrific nutrients.

823. Instead of relying on canned soups, learn how easy it is to make super healthy more nutritious soups at home.

824. Never leave a candle burning unattended.

825. Keep all cooling and heating vents clear of furniture and clean or replace the filters as needed.

826. Be sure that your dog gets plenty of exercise every day.

827. Switch out your old desktop to a laptop. Laptops use 90% less energy.

828. Make your own DIY green house.

829. Save your wine corks and make a bulletin board and other fun crafts.

830. Make simple draft stoppers for underneath your doors.

831. Save the bottom stalk of the celery to re-grow again. Place the base of the celery in a shallow bowl with water. Once the leaves start to come up, plant in soil.

832. You can re-grow green onions, lettuce, carrots, bok choy, ginger, pineapple, onions, garlic, basil, sweet potatoes and potatoes. Learn more about kitchen scrap gardening to save money.

833. If you are going through tough times always remember the caterpillar, the metamorphosis and the emerging butterfly.

834. Learn how to do sign language and visit community centers, nursing homes, and hospitals and volunteer to help the deaf or mute.

835. Like Steve Jobs, create a stress-free uniform. Why not just stick to a black t-shirt and jeans for the minimal fashion lifestyle.

836. Set a goal of reading one book a week or challenge yourself to read more.

837. Make bat houses. Bats are an integral part of our planet's ecosystem.

838. If you have come to terms with a destructive habit, just stop it.

839. Learn about energy medicine and chakras.

840. Moisturize your skin after every shower with organic coconut oil.

841. Do a weekly re-boot or more often during the week of just going outside in nature and focusing on the colors, the beauty, the wildlife and breath in the luscious clean fresh air.

842. Change your DNA with sound frequencies of 528 Hz and your personal vibration. There are many terrific resources online.

843. Listen to the ancient chants from the Buddhist and Gregorian monks. They are designed to shift your frequency.

844. Perception starts with awareness. How are you feeling right now and how can you raise your vibration. Tune in and focus on your solarplexis more often.

845. Pay attention to synchronicities and be grateful for them.

846. Get a journal and start writing your thoughts, your passions and your dreams.

847. You have thousands of neurons, which are recruited to physically write down a thought instead of just typing it into a computer. This stimulates your body, mind and soul which, sparks more enlightenment, desire and joy. This also helps with activating your creativity even more.

848. Bake or make some yummy healthy goodies for your neighbors.

849. Think of everything you really love and write it down. Super charge this action by doing it daily.

850. Take the stress out of traveling by sending a trunk of your big bulky items ahead of time, that way you can just travel with a light backpack to your destination.

851. When you are traveling listen to audio books.

852. Stimulate your mind daily by saying to yourself that you are open to receiving all things that are good, you are prosperous, you are loving, you are loved and willing to go with the flow and change.

853. Charge every single thing you do with love. If you are cooking in the kitchen think and feel loving thoughts of how this meal will nourish you and your family.

854. Take an adventure travel vacation.

855. Be sure to add clove to your weekly diet. Cloves are a terrific antioxidant, contains eugenol, which boosts the immune system, stimulates the blood circulation and purifies.

856. Take a raw food preparation class and expand your knowledge of the benefits of eating a whole food plant based diet. If you don't have the time or resources, just jump online and you will find a variety of terrific short demonstration videos on how to help you prepare easy, simple and fast nutrient dense meals for you and your family.

857. Drink energy charged water. Place the word "love" on glasses and/or glass containers. You can also hold the water with your middle fingers and thumbs touching on either side of the bottle or glass and sending the water love.

858. Don't use toxic air fresheners. It's easy and cheaper to make your own yummy delish smelling scents with water and a few drops of your favorite essential oils in a spray bottle.

859. Snuggle more.

860. Learn how to make your own hot sauces and salsas and give them as gifts in those jars you've been saving. There are lots of easy recipes online that are fun to make and much healthier without all the added preservatives.

861. Always remember that people do things for love or lack of love.

862. Set your intentions to help heal Mother Earth daily.

863. Start saving those hefty pet food bags and other sturdy container bags and learn how to make funky recycled pet food bag purses and totes. Use for grocery shopping and they make terrific gifts.

864. Always clean the lint trap in your dryer machine after each use. A dirty lint filter can use 30 percent more energy to get the job done.

865. During the week, periodically sanitize your toothbrushes by rinsing with hydrogen peroxide to kill those nasty germs. This will help keep you healthier also.

866. For a nice clean shave, just use olive oil or coconut oil. No need to purchase shaving cream.

867. While you are shaving don't keep the tap water running.

868. If you are commuting daily to work and back, why not listen to audio or self-improvement books to keep your brain engaged and learning new thoughts. You could even be learning a new language.

869. Respect all differences. Embrace ethnic groups, religions, cultures, different races and traditions. Learn to be free from discrimination.

870. Switch to biodegradable detergents. Bleaches and phosphates threaten river and marine life.

871. Install better, more efficient showerheads to reduce water usage.

872. Don't buy new chew toys for your pets. Why not take an old dishtowel or item of clothing you are no longer wearing and create new toys for your pets.

873. Time to break away from the material world to gain a new harmonious balance with the spiritual world that is emerging.

874. Be gentle on your car. Speeding, fast accelerations and hard breaking wastes gas and it's hard on your vehicle. Maintaining your car improves the overall efficiency and will last longer.

875. Purchase only organic cottons.

876. Choose biodegradable cat litter.

877. Slash packaging. When buying produce skip using the extra plastic bag for each item. You are going to go home and clean with the vinegar and water solution anyway.

878. Learn to make your own paper. It's easy and simple and can be terrific gifts.

879. Create a vision board to inspire you daily.

880. Make your own easy and inexpensive eye shadow. Use an arrow root or organic corn starch base and use raw cacao powder or make your own beet powder and use spirulina, turmeric and cinnamon.

881. For something less toxic for you and the planet, why not try to make your own chemical free natural black eye liner. All you need is activated charcoal capsules, a glass jar with a tight lid and a thin paintbrush. Open the capsules and fill up your little jar. You can use this as a smokey eye shadow or mix a little with water and use as an eyeliner.

882. Using the same activated black charcoal you can make your own mascara. Just mix with a bit of melted coconut oil and melted

bayberry wax, carnauba wax or beeswax. Clean up an old mascara brush or purchase a new mascara brush and container at the beauty supply store. Now you have a non-toxic mascara for you and the planet.

883.   Make a short list of your "things to do" to keep you on task.

884.   If you really want to get your life and home organized plan a 30 day one small task a day chore and see how easy it is to un-clutter.

885.   Don't support zoos, circuses, sea-life parks or any shows that exploit animals.

886.   Make your own easy and inexpensive dog treats with the pulp left over from your juicing, ground up flax seeds and peanut butter. Bake in the dehydrator or oven. If you don't have pets you can use the pulp and add to your soup stocks or make crackers.

887.   Make your own natural vanilla extract with vanilla beans and vodka. Take a vanilla bean and cut down the middle and place in a glass jar and fill with 4 ounces vodka. Soak for 2 months before using.

888.   Share this book with others. ☺

889.   Make your own natural and organic baby food. It's simple, much healthier and less expensive. Be sure to place the prepared food into clean glass containers and store in the refrigerator. Rotate often.

890.   Outside, place organic apples, nuts and seeds to help feed the local wildlife.

891.   There is simply no need for fabric softeners. Simply use ½ cup white vinegar in the last rinse cycle in your washing machine.

892.   Stop buying anti-wrinkle creams full of toxic chemicals. Make your own by melting some beeswax, coconut oil, let cool a bit and add some rosehip-seed-oil and rose water. Mix well and place in glass jar.

893.   Stay away from canola, corn and vegetable oils. They are most likely GMO's and if you are heating at high temperatures they will oxidize and cause inflammation and clogged arteries. Your best bet is to always use coconut oil, especially for high heat cooking.

894. Make your own chemical free homemade mayonnaise. Using a blender, blend 2 eggs, 1 tablespoon organic apple cider vinegar, ¾ teaspoon salt and 2 teaspoons mustard, blend well and then very slowly drizzle in 2 cups olive oil, blend up well. Will keep in frig for up to 2 weeks. If you are a vegan, another simple recipe for mayonnaise is ½ cup of nut milk, ½ teaspoon sea salt (or less), 1 teaspoon ground mustard, 1 ½ teaspoons garlic powder, 2 teaspoons apple cider vinegar, 2 teaspoons agave nectar or a dash of Stevia, 1 cup organic melted coconut oil and place all in blender and place in glass jar and store in the refrigerator for up to a week.

895. Don't drink sodas, diet sodas, or anything with chemicals in it.

896. Avoid any type of food coloring and additives. Many studies have proven the harmful affects of these toxic chemicals.

897. Make your own chemical free ketchup. Blend 1 ½ cups organic chopped tomatoes, 3 pitted dates, ¼ cup olive oil, 1 teaspoon sea salt, 1 tablespoon organic apple cider vinegar blend well and then add ½ cup sun dried tomatoes. Place in glass jar and place in the refrigerator.

898. Don't purchase anything that has corn syrup or high fructose corn syrup in it.

899. For a once in a while splurge make your own chemical free Nutella. Just place all the ingredients in a food processor and blend well. First roast the hazelnuts at 375 degrees for about 12 minutes. Let cool. Combine 8 ounces of hazelnuts, ½ cups raw organic honey, ½ cup raw cacao powder, 2 tablespoons of melted coconut oil, 1 teaspoon vanilla, 1 teaspoon salt. Place in glass jar and in the refrigerator.

900. Always wash your new clothes before wearing them. There are many toxic chemicals used as finishing agents on fabric.

901. Make your own chemical free scented candles. Melt beeswax and add your favorite essential oils and slowly pour into a clean glass jar with wick.

902. Save those used coffee grounds, and use them as mulch in your acid loving plants like tomatoes and blueberries. You can also spread the used coffee grounds on a cookie sheet and place them in the oven to dry them out and add them to the kitty litter box to absorb odors.

903. Use generous amounts of black pepper on your dishes. The benefits include help with digestion, prevents gas, promotes sweating, relieves joint pain, promotes healthy skin, relieves coughs and colds, antibacterial, keeps arteries clean, and great antioxidant.

904. Stop wishing and start doing.

905. Instead of buying store bought jams, just buy fresh berries (soak and clean well with the vinegar and water method) and blend them up in your blender with a bit of honey and a squeeze of lemon juice. Eat right away or store in a glass jar in the refrigerator.

906. What ever you decide to do, always make sure it makes you happy.

907. Always be brave.

908. Live less out of habit and more out of intent.

909. Think about what you are doing today to make a better world tomorrow.

910. Screw trying to empress other people.

911. Stop using toxic sunscreen and make your own awesome natural lotion by melting ¼ cup coconut oil, ¼ cup melted beeswax, ½ cup olive oil, 2 tablespoons zinc oxide, 1 teaspoons red raspberry seed oil, 1 teaspoon carrot seed oil, 1 teaspoon vitamin E oil, 1 or 2 drops of lavender oil. Mix well and place in glass jar and in the refrigerator. Good up to 6 months.

912. The sign of a beautiful person is they always see beauty in others.

913. Expect nothing and appreciate everything.

914. Fall in love with as many things as possible.

915. Always remember you are stronger than you think.

916. You can't out exercise a poor diet. Next time you eat something that is high in calories know that a workout at the gym isn't going to fix what you just ate.

917. Don't purchase dryer sheets. They are chock full of toxic chemicals.

918. Be sure to add more peppers into your diet. Hot and spicy, fresh or dried, they are terrific in helping to lower the risk of skin and colon cancers, anti-microbial, detoxifying, good for the heart and skin, and the compound capsaicin is a powerhouse of aiding to help rebuild tissues in the stomach and intestines, boosts circulation, helps with stiff arthritic joints, relieves nerve pain and strengthens digestion.

919. If you think making change is hard then it is.

920. If you think making change is easy then it is.

921. Learn about water and juice fasting and re-set your system. It's an easy way to re-set all of your magical taste buds and get you easily back on track to a healthier and thinner you.

922. Avoid MSG – Monosodium Glutamate. Jump online and learn all the secret ways they label this unhealthy chemical food additive.

923. Always wear shower flip-flops in public swimming areas. As a matter of fact, always pack them for traveling and wear them in your hotel room.

924. Don't drink tea and coffee with your meals. The tannins will prevent you from absorbing certain minerals and iron.

925. Do more of what makes you awesome.

926. Be the type of person you want to meet.

927. Eat more pineapple. It contains anti-inflammatory enzymes that bring pain relief to arthritis.

928. Eat more curry, the curcumin compounds can help stop amyloid plaques that cause Alzheimer's.

929. Onions are natural antibiotics. Be sure to add to your dishes and salads. However don't plan on adding them to your potluck dishes, because when onions are left out for several hours they can cause food poisoning.

930. Lots of uses for hydrogen peroxide, such as cleaning mold, sanitizing, foot fungus, canker sores, toothpaste, prevent infections, whitening clothes, hair lightener, and glass cleaner.

931. Realize that some people can remain in your heart but not in your life.

932. Make your own natural pet shampoo with baking soda and white vinegar.

933. Learn about food combining to help you digest your meals much easier and maximize the nutrients, vitamins and minerals.

934. Have a bug-out backpack always ready for an emergency.

935. Never walk alone in an alley or drive alone in bad areas.

936. Make your own natural lip balm with melted beeswax, cocoa butter, and coconut oil and add fun tints like cocoa powder, cinnamon, turmeric, and essential oils. Place in small tins.

937. There is always time to change the road you are on.

938. Kiwi fruit can improve your eyesight. They are full of lutein and antioxidants.

939. Always keep your head up, walk with confidence and swing those arms.

940. Limit fizzy drinks. The tartrazine found in fizzy drinks causes depletion of zinc levels. Zinc plays a vital role in supporting our immune system.

941. Purchase a really great personal water filtration system that will make emergency drinking water safe. Consider having several, one for your bug-out backpack and for your car.

942. Always be aware of your surroundings and avoid placing yourself in danger.

943. Know some cancer basics. We all have cancer cells and keeping your body in a more alkaline state and not over indulging on sugar, meats/animal proteins (which include dairy) will help. Cancer is a disease of the mind, body and spirit. Work on keeping that energy flowing more positively.

944. Understand the difference of bad fat versus good fats. Omega-3's are the healthy fats that your brain and body needs. Olives, avocados, nuts, and seeds are all terrific sources.

945. You have a daily choice of growth or decay.

946. Step away from exercise machines, your body is the machine.

947. Remind yourself how far you've come.

948. Take a ceramics class.

949. Let go of past trauma and wounds.

950. Invest in a good switchblade knife or army knife and carry with you at all times.

951. Embrace and love what makes you different.

952. Drink more coconut water.

953. Stop smoking chemical laden and cancer causing cigarettes. You know this isn't good for you or your family and pets.

954. Try not to use your hair dryer that often to reduce your exposure to EMF's – Electromagnetic Fields are very dangerous to your health and not to mention the heat damage to your hair. The high wattage from usage of the hair dryers are also staggering. Opt for a fun hairstyle that will dry gorgeously on it's own.

955. Get in touch with your inner dialog. What are you saying to yourself?

956. Try a new sport or recreational activity.

957. Spend quality time with your parents and family.

958. Search for a few of your favorite inspirational quotes and post them up on your wall.

959. Get your daily requirement of calcium by eating lots of leafy greens, figs, sesame seeds, beans, blackstrap molasses or almonds.

960. Don't believe everything you think

961. Learn how to get by on the bare minimum.

962. Remember not to believe everything you read or hear. Go with that gut feeling.

963. Learn about Diatomaceous Earth and how it can help with high cholesterol, hair growth, fleas, de-worming pets, bed bugs and toenail fungus.

964. Buy a dry body brush and brush your skin to get rid of dead skin cells, stimulate the lymph system and help the body rid itself of toxins, and increase circulation and energy.

965. Know it's never too late to get your shit together.
966. Remember that people will either love or hate you and none of it will have anything to do with you.
967. Wrap your water heater in an insulating jacket.
968. Be impeccable with your words.
969. Learn to apologize. Show strength by admitting your mistakes or wrong doings.
970. Create a nice and tidy working space that will keep your head clear and focused.
971. Vacuum or clean the back of your coils on your refrigerator.
972. Be sure to add cumin to your dishes or soups because it's a terrific anti-inflammatory and antioxidant that may also help stop tumor growth.
973. Master body weight movements before adding weight resisted movements.
974. The object of personal fitness is to fully support your daily activities.
975. Don't eat a heavy dinner right before going to bed. Make sure you allow 3-4 hours of digestion.
976. Allow yourself to constantly adapt to change.
977. Always do your best and do what you can.
978. See the future not as something to be fearful of but to embrace the magic and opportunity.
979. Don't be reckless with other people's hearts and don't put up with people who are reckless with yours.
980. Be a master of whatever you do. Eliminate mediocrity from your life.
981. Life is the coexistence of all opposite values. This planet is 3rd dimensional and always remember we live in a constant shifting of joy and sorrow and of birth and death.
982. Just say no to anything with Aspartame or Amino Sweet in it.
983. Make an art form of nonconformity.

984. Have all of your mercury fillings removed and replaced with much safer fillings.

985. Avoid personal care products that advertise use of nanotechnology.

986. Be careful of "green-washing" products stating they are organic or natural. Read the labels and synthetic petrochemicals or other harmful carcinogens.

987. Don't use hair straighteners or get perms, they are made from formaldehyde and ammonium thioglycolate, which is extremely toxic, harmful and causes many unseen health issues. Embrace your natural beauty and make the best out of what you are born with.

989. Rinse rice well and pre-soak over night before cooking to reduce cooking time.

990. If we don't include fundamental movement patterns throughout the day, we will loose them.

991. If you are pregnant, to keep you and the baby super healthy, make sure to eat whole plant based foods such as organic Non-GMO vegetables, fruits, whole grains, legumes, drink nut milks, drink plenty of clean filtered water. Avoid all processed junk food and drinks. Keep moving and exercising and get plenty of rest.

992. Don't use toxic chemicals to get rid of rust. You can do this inexpensively with just a little baking soda, vinegar and lemon juice. Just make this into a paste, rub onto the rusty metal and allow the solution to dry and rub off with steel wool.

993. Do your homework regarding name brands that are using sweatshops, child labor, or unfair labor practices. Educate others and boycott these companies. We must all work together to stop these unfair exploitations.

994. Join the global communities supporting clean free water for all.

995. Treat everybody like it's his or her birthday.

996. Human Trafficking is a global issue of great concern. Join grassroots causes and help others to increase their awareness, helping put an end this form of slavery.

997. Get out of breath several times a day. Either by running up the stairs, walking vigorously or by just even doing jumping jacks or Tabata squats. Keep moving.

998. Leave a little sparkle wherever you go.

999. As we get older learning about balance and fall prevention by being aware of your center of gravity and maintaining your base of support.

1000. Learn from the past, set vivid detailed goals for the future and take charge of living in the now.

1001. Treat your Mother Earth like the magical planet that she is, walk lightly, and honor her. We must hold the intention of preserving it for our children's children and all it's inhabitants.

ABOUT ME

Hello! I'm Judy Wong Dobberpuhl, now an Eco-Peaceful-Warrior. I came from Nada to Prada and now a fun loving Earth Mama. Raised in a first generation Chinese-American family of five, I learned from my parents how to make the best of every situation. Growing up, I spent a lot of time alone making crafts in my room and loved to bake and sew, to see what I could create. I was always intrigued with gardening and growing plants from seeds. I learned to play piano, then the guitar, and even dabbled with playing the drums. I have always been an animal lover, finding compassion as a much-needed trait for successful daily living and loving.

I had a super fun, lucrative career in finance and sales for 33 years. I was lucky to make some great friends and see a lot of the world. One day I awoke to realize that I used to rage against the machine, and that I had now become part of the machine. (Yes, a heavy metal chick.). I dove head long into senseless consumerism based on status and feeding my ego. It became an unfulfilling cycle of mass credit card debt that I was constantly burdened with. My addiction to online shopping and my need for retail therapy left me wanting more and more. It also didn't help my fashion addiction, by attending fashion design and merchandising college, in the evenings, after my day job. It only seemed to increase my desire for designer clothing and accessories. Now I can say, "Been there, done that" and now I'm just left with the designer T-shirt.

Luckily, I started spending thousands of hours reading, researching, and watching documentaries, uncovering the lies and manipulations of the monetary system. Once you unplug from the matrix, you can't go back. My husband and I got rid of most of our material possessions, and quit our jobs, to leave the never-ending rat race and explore the conscious awakening shift.

I attended a terrific progressive raw food culinary school, Living Light Culinary School in Fort Bragg, California and received my Gourmet Raw Food and Raw Food Educator Certifications. I am also a big fan of Dr. T. Colin Campbell and enthusiastically took his eCornell course on Plant Based Nutrition. I have always enjoyed learning about health and wellness and staying super healthy. I love reading and learning as much as I can and also helping others. I have a very strong belief that we are on this planet to love and help others. I have done a few triathlons, half marathons and even taught aerobics and indoor spin classes. I was always passionate about teaching fitness classes and loved getting to know everyone and their journey to wellness. Passion has always fueled my desire to really dive into the truth of body, mind and spirit.

We now live a very simple life of less with our two rescue dogs and two cats. We are traveling and volunteering currently in South America. The goal is to see the world and dive into the many colorful cultures, amazing geography and culinary experiences around us.

My inspirations, experiences, and follies from my career have led me to writing this book. I've learned that people like learning in smaller chunks, love life hacks, and motivational tidbits. I have written this book for the audience that loves easy tips, that are looking to make their lives richer, and to help save our planet for all that inhabit this beautiful blue sphere. I've stumbled a lot, made mistakes, and I keep getting up and learning to make it all a part of the life dance.

My goal is to motivate you to make going back to basics and supporting the slow food movement, one of the coolest and hippest things you can do. I challenge you to ask more questions and learn different ways to keep you and your family healthier, wiser and loving. Let's rediscover a simpler lifestyle and cast off the over consumption model that modern living has brought us. Once we shed this core belief that we must keep this unsustainable lifestyle choice up, we begin to open to new opportunities for truly sustainable living. Our planet doesn't have infinite resources, so waking up to this paradigm shift is paramount. I know in my heart we can all get fairly close to getting back to zero-waste living.

I have written this fun book to help you take back your power. Realize that your mind is your greatest asset and be the unique magical you that you are meant to be. Know that you can make a difference. Fill your precious heart with love and let it spill over.

Sending you love, bliss, light and truth. Free Your Mind. Namaste.